MW00770845

The Chasers

THE CHASERS

Renato Rosaldo

DUKE UNIVERSITY PRESS · DURHAM AND LONDON · 2019

Designed by Matthew Tauch
Typeset in Garamond Premier Pro
by Westchester Publishing Services

Library of Congress Cataloging-in-Publication Data
Names: Rosaldo, Renato, author.
Title: The chasers
Description: Durham : Duke University Press, 2019. |
Includes bibliographical references and index.
Identifiers: LCCN 2018050152 (print) |
LCCN 2018059394 (ebook) |
ISBN 9781478005643 (ebook) |
ISBN 9781478004189 (hardcover : alk. paper) |
ISBN 9781478004776 (pbk. : alk. paper)
Subjects: | LCGFT: Poetry.
Classification: LCC PS3618.O775 (ebook) |
LCC PS3618.O775 C44 2019 (print) |
DDC 811/.6—dc23
LC record available at https://lccn.loc.gov
/2018050152

Cover art: Photo of Chasers members, *Tucsonian*,
Tucson High School, 1959

To the memory of

MY FATHER, RENATO ROSALDO;

MY MOTHER, BETTY POTTER ROSALDO;

MY GRANDMOTHER, MAMA EMILIA

Contents

Prelude

How to imagine the Chasers? A band of twelve high school guys, more club than gang. Their jackets made them visible at Tucson High, 1956–1959.

Eleven were Mexican-American, one Jewish. Ethnicity was trumped. You were or were not a Chaser.

I was a Chaser.

You're about to read an auto-ethnography. It's personal. It's about what it meant to be a Chaser, how it sustained us, how we sustained us, how they sustained me.

It could be seen as historical ethnography, a portrait of a small group, except that the purpose of what I learned through participant-observation was not social description.

It was personal.

My intention was to go native, become Mexican-American, not to write it up. To deepen my humanity. And I did.

After meeting up for our fiftieth Tucson High School reunion, we Chasers remembered what we never forgot, what we held close, the people and places we never let go.

Little wonder that, once we resumed, we couldn't stop gathering, looking back, unforgetting.

Poetry revived memories of my feelings. Personal losses gave me vital perceptions. Collective recollections of bygone camaraderie opened me to this book.

Cast of Characters

THE CHASERS

Andy Contreras, supermarket produce manager, deceased, Tucson, AZ

Dickie Cota-Robles, HVAC southern Arizona field superintendent for a mechanical contractor, Tucson, AZ

Louie Dancil, marijuana smuggler, Tucson, AZ

Dickie Delahanty, fireman and paramedic, Tucson, AZ

Ray Escalante, artist, singer, U.S.-Mexico border

Ralph "Ginger" Estrada, lawyer, Phoenix, AZ

Frank Howe, elementary school principal, Tucson, AZ

Richard Koenig, M.D., psychiatrist, East Quogue, NY

Freddie Ochoa, estimator, moving and storage, Pinetop, AZ

Richard Rocha, lawyer, Tucson, AZ

Renato "Chico"/"Chato" Rosaldo, professor, cultural
anthropology, Stanford and New York University,
Brooklyn, NY

Bobby Shoumaker, M.D., neurologist, San Antonio, TX

ANGLO FRIENDS OF THE CHASERS

Neal Manning, realtor, Tucson, AZ

John Warnock, professor of English, Writing & Rhetoric,
University of Arizona, Tucson, AZ

WOMAN FRIEND OF THE CHASERS

Angie López, elementary and middle school teacher of
Spanish, owner of religious store, Tucson, AZ

I

• FRANK HOWE •

Walnuts

My first day, first grade in Pirtleville, outside Douglas, kid breaks a chair, blames me. Teacher sends me to principal's office.

Older brother, Jimmy, looks in window, sees I'm crying, runs home, tells Mother who gets angry at teacher, pulls me out of school.

We move to California, follow crops—first, second, third, fourth, fifth, sixth grade. Pure survival. I lose two years of school.

At labor camp—one faucet, one outhouse, one stove. We Mexican migrant kids bused to school, dropped in cafeteria, given paper and crayons, brought back to fields for lunch.

Mother brings burritos and I feel happy. We work until five or six. Being with family is good.

The money's in walnuts, but Jimmy and I pick apricots and tomatoes, bending over. Backaches. Dad picks oranges and lemons.

By grade six we settle in Tucson, but that summer we go back to California's walnuts. Dad takes a pole with hook at one end, shakes walnuts from trees.

Jimmy and I collect as fast as we can, fill gunny sacks, dump, make piles. Mother follows, sits, peels green husks, drops them in buckets.

Back to Tucson, school's already started.

Frank Howe

Never Chicano Enough

Young people in MeCHa, organ of the Chicana/o student movement, flaunt badges of belonging: East L.A., farmworker, gang member.

A daughter of farmworkers, fingers thick from picking crops, English accented, appears Chicana to the max, but she feels like a phony, her Spanish lost to shame during grade school.

As a faculty member I embrace my self-portrait as a Chaser, my Chicano badge of honor, before it was convenient.

Fifty years of icon-clouded memories. Can't sort what I invented from what I remember or what I lived—who we were, what we did. I cling to the remnant of authenticity that hangs in my bedroom closet—my Chasers jacket.

Chico Rosaldo

• RENATO ROSALDO •

Suddenly Blank

Summers in Mexico City I play, speaking Spanish with my cousins: Jaime, Héctor, Edgar, Irma.

At home, in Madison, I speak English with Mom, Spanish with Dad. When I'm four, Mom and Dad show me off to their friends, let me speak English, ask me to speak Spanish. On display, I cringe, feeling out of place.

Every day after school, on Dad's lap, I unfold my day in Spanish. Then, at six years of age, I talk about my visit to the zoo, the word "elefante" gone, utterly gone.

It's as if Spanish is a screen that flickers, turns off, suddenly blank. Now I am like the other Madison kids.

The pain, as if my tongue yanked out by the root. A piece of me gone.

Chico Rosaldo

Nice Meals

One morning I ask Mom to put mustard on my bologna sandwich 'cause that's how Willie likes them. Mom sputters. My cheeks blister.

Fifty years later, Neal Manning asks if I remember Willie Cocio, the bean burritos his mom made.

Back in grade school Neal and Willie traded lunches. Then at Mansfeld Junior High, it was my turn.

My mother had bragging rights. Her sandwiches won me those tasty bartered legends.

This story mutated her embarrassment to bologna and mustard pride.

Neal Manning and Chico Rosaldo

Down the Little Arroyo

I looked older than the other guys, so I'd buy the beer at a small Chinese store in the desert by the old hospital west of St. Mary's.

We'd go down Anklam, turn right on a dirt road we'd been smart enough to scout.

We said if cops came we'd go down the little arroyo, drive up, go across, come back on Anklam, then head back to town on a road that went north along a wide arroyo to Speedway.

We'd cruise there, real slow, cross, then speed up.

One time, it happened, the cops came. The guys went west, down the little arroyo, their lights on and, boom, got stuck in the arroyo.

Dickie Delahanty

• DICKIE DELAHANTY •

Never Dreamed

FRANK:

You wrote me while I was in Guam. Yeah, writing, we inspired each other. All positive.

CHICO:

The letters mattered, the writing. It felt like my going to college gave you confidence. You said, "I can do that. If Chico can do it, I can do it."

FRANK:

I took your dad's class in Mexican culture. He gave me an A. I enjoyed your dad because of the way he lectured. He was funny. He had nothing in front of him, everything from the top of his head, a huge class, no podium. He'd walk, everybody listening.

CHICO:

Mexican history and culture were in his heart. He led tours of Mexico, spent time in places he lectured about, that history lived in buildings and stories he knew intimately.

FRANK:

You came from a more cultured home environment than I.
My parents never talked about, never even dreamed of going
to New York City, Mexico City, or Guam.

At home all was survival. My dad worked in the moving busi-
ness, my mother was a housewife and worked at St. Mary's
Hospital. Just survival, never dreamed, the furthest they
went was L.A.

Frank Howe and Chico Rosaldo

A Dark Side

Kay Barnhill and Patti Dunlap were in a clique, the in-group. They started dating Bobby and Dickie, made the Chasers more visible.

Back then Tucson High included the whole city. It was the end of an era, high schools became smaller, neighborhood schools, more segregated.

You've said how picking up and dropping off the guys was a Chaser ritual, drove the city end to end, took all night. In the car: banter, hard-assing.

At our fiftieth reunion we Anglos celebrated the Chasers. There was a sense of pathways. We thought of our school as a blackboard jungle.

You could do Okay or become a juvenile delinquent. Certain signs told whether you were going one way or the other.

I didn't have the burden of having to look cool, reducing visible signs of being a good student. I could carry books in the halls.

People thought the Chasers would go the other way, that you'd chosen the delinquent pathway.

People at the reunion were delighted you'd done so well. It wasn't so much an expectation, as a worry, about how you'd turn out. A sense you were on the wrong path, a dark side.

It may have been a cold war mentality, the world divided into a dark side and a bright side. There was the rebel without a cause, drag racing around town, flirting with death.

Remember Gene Puga, just beautiful, his hair almost blue, handsome, wasn't going to make it. The story, I heard later: he stole a police car, drove around taunting the cops.

Life can turn out different ways: Gene Puga, one way, the Chasers, another. Seeing the Chasers gave our class a heightened sense of possibility.

John Warnock

· JOHN WARNOCK ·

Talking with Mom

MOM SAYS,

Our anthropologist friend, Jim Officer, is an expert on Mexican-American teenage gangs in Tucson. He says what you, Chato, have done by joining the Chasers is remarkable. It never happens.

CHATO SAYS,

He gets to be called an expert by talking to guys like us Chasers. We're the real experts.

MOM SAYS,

Jim tells me that only Tucson-born kids can join Mexican-American gangs and only a brother or a cousin can become a member, not someone unrelated.

CHATO SAYS,

He thinks we're following rules, but, remember, we're making it up as we go along.

MOM SAYS,

The Chasers are so much fun. They decorate our house for their parties, tape crepe paper streamers to the ceiling: yellow, purple, green.

CHATO SAYS,

They're nice guys. I'm glad you really like them.

MOM SAYS,

They play music and dance. So lively. They talk with me and your dad. So polite. Call us sir and ma'am.

CHATO SAYS,

They're polite with other people's parents.

Chico Rosaldo

• RAY ESCALANTE •

Fastest Naked Sprinter

We had swimming parties at El Encanto Estates. We'd scout, see who's on vacation, and use their pool.

One time, when we were there, Ray forgot his trunks, the beachcombers we wore. Ray didn't have any. We were swimming when somebody called the cops.

They came and we took off running. They threw on the spotlight and there was Ray running across the street bare-ass naked.

One morning at Shannon's house, her parents took off for the day. Ray lived across the street. He saw the car leave and went over.

They're doing shenanigans when her parents come back and Shannon comes out in a bathrobe.

Her dad goes in the bedroom, opens the closet door and there's Ray. He takes off across the street bare-ass naked.

Ray and Shannon got into an argument. He sped off, rolled that old green thing, flipped it on the corner.

We ran there, Shannon hysterical, Ray stood up, saying, like he did, "Oh, Jesus."

Dickie Delahanty

In the Cactus Chronicle

THE TUCSON HIGH NEWSPAPER

"I'd say we turned out average. We span the spectrum.
Some exceeded expectations, some didn't."

—BOBBY SHOUMAKER

The Chasers told stories when they reunited at the Shanty fifty years after graduation. They were a social club with rambunctious football players. Many were neighbors, have known each other since grade school.

When they attended school, they were seen as the "bad guys." They were the ones invited to crash parties, and they were the troublemakers.

The reunion started when a member in New York contacted Dickie Cota-Robles. It snowballed from there and ten of the original twelve members attended. Two were not located in time.

After high school, two worked as lawyers and one each as a neurosurgeon, a singer, and a school principal. Rosaldo received a scholarship to Harvard and is now a renowned anthropologist.

The Chasers hope to get together again and include the two members who weren't present.

Dylan Barnes (Faculty Advisor)

The Chaser Mystique

Most said we'd turn out badly.

Our name signified wild guy, partier, fighter. We thrived on reputation. Whether they admired or hated us, everyone knew who we were, our jackets, our spot in the stairwell.

We played the cat, built a mystique, but we were just Mexican kids out for fun, nothing profound.

One dad in moving and storage, Chico's dad a professor, another selling beer at ball games, another a cop, and yet another, head of a rotating credit association, the Alianza Hispanoamericana.

We were in shape, every summer our arms threw baseballs, our backs strained under bulky furniture. One worked as a lifeguard.

We hadn't seen each other for fifty years, gathered at the Tucson High School reunion, told ourselves stories about ourselves, laughed as if we'd been together the day before.

At our reunion, people still talked about us, still gave a shit after fifty years.

Bobby Shoumaker and Richard Rocha

II

Playing Ball

I was one of the original Chasers. The others were Bobby Shoumaker and Dickie Cota-Robles. I went to Roskruge Junior High with Bobby, started hanging out, used to meet at Menlo Park.

Then it just started developing. Richard Rocha and my neighbor, Andy Contreras, were originals too.

I don't recall how some of the other guys came on, like yourself and Louie Dancil.

Ralph Estrada was one of the originals. I think he brought in Koenig, his neighbor. Freddy Ochoa came through his neighbor, Dickie Cota-Robles.

We were on the football team: Bobby, myself, Ray Escalante, Dickie Delahanty, one of the quarterbacks.

I was a center. Bobby was an end and so was Ray. Ralph was small, really tough, played defensive back, took no prisoners, gutsy. The core of the Chasers was football and other sports.

Personally, I joined the Navy Reserve in January of '58, boot camp in San Diego the summer between my junior and senior year. When I came back, Bobby and I hung out.

He'd come over to my place in Menlo Park. We'd get ready for football, run up "A" mountain. We started doing the Chaser thing, hanging out.

Ralph had a '53 Chevy, would pick me up at home in Menlo Park. Bobby'd come to Barrio Hollywood, blowing his horn.

We'd jump in the car and go buy beer in Hollywood, at the little Chinese stores. Delahanty'd buy and the Chinese people'd sell the booze. We'd speed off. Away we'd go.

Frank Howe

Sports People

You Chasers were a band of brothers, a fraternity, so close, and you've started again.

You Chasers were smart, kept it secret, two sets of books, never looked like nerds, nobody messed with you.

I know what you were up against. When I taught at Sunnyside, the best students were shamed, called "school boy" and "school girl." The jealousy, the jealousy.

That's why I was shocked to learn Bobby became a neurologist; Richard and Ralph, lawyers; Koenig, a psychiatrist; you, professor of anthropology.

You Chasers were sports people, five on the football team, you, captain of the swim team, others played baseball and basketball. Anglo girls went after you.

Tom King said Anglo boys felt jealous, wondered why you crashed their parties, didn't know the girls had invited you.

I've always wondered why you went steady with me, a Mexican girl. Most Chasers dated Anglo girls.

At your parties, you danced with your dates, not like Mexicans, guys on one side, girls on the other. There was a lot of respect for us girls.

There was loyalty, everyone had your back. It wasn't spoken, it just was.

Angie López

All about Fun

The Belmonts, Gaylords, Vikings, and Playboys all had jackets. Without jackets we Chasers were nothing.

Dickie came up with the design for our jackets, a glass with booze, big and all. We looked for the jacket at Dave Bloom & Sons. Don't remember how we paid, but each one paid.

We were proud when we wore them at school, but they said, "Forget you." George Hunt was cold, just said, "No, you guys can't be wearing this at school."

We still wore them around town, but not on campus. It was a fun time, all about fun, just hanging out, partying, not paying too much attention, some of us paid no attention to education.

When my senior year counselor Curtis Anderson asked, "What are you going to do after you graduate?" I said, "I'm already in the Navy, then I'm going to college. Am I all set?" He said, "You're all set."

That year I took three courses: wood shop, government, and English. Then at noon I played music on the phonograph in the cafeteria where the ladies would give me their food. That was fun.

I didn't accomplish a single project in wood shop. Hard to focus. I was thinking only about trading my jacket for a uniform, dreaming of seeing the world, of meeting girls.

Graduated Tucson High, June 7th, 1959, then went on active duty July 7th, was overseas for all my tour, twenty-four months, Guam, Okinawa, the Philippines, Japan.

I didn't like the Philippines, Okinawa was nice, Guam was very nice. I went to college in Guam. That's the way you met girls, but I somehow picked up six hours of college credit.

The women in Guam were really pretty, a mixture of Japanese, Portuguese, Spanish, Filipina, unique look, pretty girls.

Frank Howe

• DEAN HUNT •

A Quiet Guy

I do the Chasers thing, hang out in the stairwell, studiously casual, nod chin slightly upward, greeting friends. I watch the others, their chin-lifts, my imitation precise.

Determined to re-learn Spanish (for me a matter of pride), I do relentless grammar drills, make Mexican history mine, read Los de Abajo as well as Pedro Páramo. So bookish, busting ass to be Mexican-American.

I observe Bobby, master of hard-assing: mock aggression, rapid-fire retorts, verbal virtuosity. If only I could be like him.

First time I give it a try, Frank pulls me aside, arm around my shoulder, says, "No more, don't do it again. You'll get in trouble. Remember it's never really about the other guy's mother."

A kid from Madison, I've never hard-assed. I feel like a phony Mexican-American, become a quiet guy, no more banter.

Chico Rosaldo

In Formation

Before school every morning
we gather, our spot in stair-
well, watch girls go by.

Hard to remember how it started. Dickie
and I talked of forming a club with
friends.

Dickie and I are cousins, our mothers are sisters.
Our bond makes the Chasers like brothers, cre-
ates camaraderie. As a group, we're go-getters,
trouble-makers.

As individuals, Dickie and I, Frank, Chico, and Freddie are
shy, reclusive, prone to blushing. The Chasers need, we need
each other.

Other groups, the Vikings, Gaylords, Belmonts, Playboys are united by blood. They're brothers and cousins.

We add new members, stop at twelve. Try to organize, elect president, vice president, but have no top, no bottom, all equal. By next morning, officers forgotten.

Our goals: crashing parties, getting in fights, hard-assing, joking, laughing.

We walk as one, blossom as one.

Bobby Shoumaker

Champagne in a Martini Glass

Our jackets make us who we are, visible, guys on the wild side.

At Dave Bloom & Sons, we look at jackets, need better than the long coats the Gaylords sport. We choose short, wool, gray.

Our name means chasing girls. I draw a guy, like little Abner, running after a skimpily dressed girl. I pass this logo by George Hunt, Dean of Boys. Get nixed.

A seamstress machine embroiders crimson letters, "Chasers" above, "Tucson" below. I design a new logo, pink champagne, three bubbles, one bursting from tilted glass, toothpick in olive.

Chasers: drinks after a glass of hard liquor, but I know nothing, only beer, nothing about mixed drinks. I put champagne in a martini glass, make our jacket unique, beautiful.

Dean Hunt stares, sees no beauty, says, "No, not on campus, no alcoholic beverage, wear your jackets anywhere in town, but never here on campus."

Dickie Cota-Robles

• DICKIE COTA-ROBLES •

• RALPH ESTRADA •

White, Black, or Blue

The Chaser organization of which I'm proud to be a member started approximately many years ago when a few of us decided to form a group. Bobby Shoumaker and Dickie Cota-Robles had the idea.

I've lived many years as a practicing attorney, and as a father of ten children. I've seen a lot from the time we were in high school.

We Chasers have a lot to be proud of. So magnificent that 90 percent of us were successful. We made a wonderful group, from different parts of town.

This isn't the lawyer talking. We owe a debt of gratitude to our parents, less because of what we did than because of what they taught us. They taught us to be proud of our roots.

They taught us something else, not taught by many people here in Tucson: don't be prejudiced, love everybody, give everybody a chance, whether they're white, black, or blue.

That made our parents special. I'm proud to be a Chaser.

Ralph Estrada

My Inner Mexican Comes In

Support from a band of brothers gives me confidence. We challenge Anglos who act like our betters. Get rid of that feeling of being inferior.

I want to show them, say, "Hell, I can pick up this white girl." Maybe I shouldn't say that out loud.

My only negative: a girl asks me to TWIRP Week dance, the day girls invite boys. My inner Mexican comes in, makes me unable to hurt her feelings. I can't say no.

I pick her up at home. Her father questions, "Are you Frank Howe?"

A nice girl, she says her daddy doesn't appreciate her going out with a Mexican. I say, "That's fine. I understand." I take her out a few times, on the sly, like Dickie with Patti.

The only ones dating Mexicans are Ginger and you, Chico. Both Dickie and Bobby have to date their girls, their forbidden fruit, on the side.

The girls probably feel the same, as if sneaking a butterscotch sundae.

Frank Howe

• FREDDIE OCHOA •

No More Oranges

One summer, high school friends challenged us Chasers to an orange fight. I remember going to Ginger's car, pulled out the back seat, filled it with oranges.

God knows where the hell we got all those oranges. Drove back to school, threw oranges everywhere. I remember the police came. Somebody said they took us to jail, but I don't remember that.

They took us to Mother Higgins, the juvie. I phoned my mom. If I told you what she said, it'd be nasty. Her fury, my being so stupid. I was one not to get in trouble.

Once I explained, my mom settled, said, "Freddie." No, no, she always called me Alfredo. Nobody else called me that. She said, "Never again, Alfredo, don't ever do that again."

I haven't. No more oranges. No more. Now I grow them. Now I eat them.

My name is Alfredo de Ochoa. As a young man I was Freddie.

Freddie Ochoa

No Emblem

I wanted to be a Chaser but was never invited. We still hung out, quality guys, more a club than gang.

Their jackets were neat. I bought one, but didn't have the emblem. People said stuff about the jackets, but it never bothered me. I knew the guys, knew the truth. Bad stuff I heard, in one ear, and out.

I remember looking out of the main building, the grounds there, somebody beating up on somebody. Everybody went on down there, a big old fight.

Jim Sickler did something to some guys. They jumped him. Then all the Chasers ran out.

I was on the second floor, saw it from a distance, a good place for me.

Neal Manning

• NEAL MANNING •

Ode to Ralph

You talk about your favorite movie, *Stand and Deliver*, how the Bolivian calculus teacher inspires his AP students to study con ganas and excel.

You forget a detail from the film.

You forget how the teacher's star pupil, a bad-ass, a pachuco, follows your lead, buys two sets of books, one for home, one for school, never carries any, nobody messes with him at Garfield High, East L.A.

You forgot your legacy to me. Let me refresh your memory.

You got A's in our biology class, but never carried the textbook. You'd read the book, memorized the definitions that were on the test: mitosis, meiosis.

You confided your secret when I asked.

You bought two sets of books, one for school, one for home. After that, I never carried books and nobody messed with me.

You redeemed my high school years. You put up my name to be a Chaser. You taught me the two-book survival skill. I owe you, Ralph.

Chico Rosaldo

I'd Like the Job

As an educator in Tucson, I had a rep: fearless, speaks truth, inspires young Chicano teachers. I don't like to brag, but what I'm saying is true.

Didn't come easy for me. Dad finished fifth grade, Mother seventh. They said schooling mattered, but couldn't help.

Went from high school to Navy, then the moving business, Ralph's Transfer, paid well in those days. Dad and a cousin worked there. Cousin taught me to drive a truck.

I passed entrance exams for university, but my certificate of admittance said I had to pick up chemistry and geometry. Talked to Curtis Anderson, my counselor, said, "What the hell? Remember me? I'm not going back to high school. You said after the Navy I'd be all set for college." He said, "I'll take care of it." And he did.

Never was a good student. In college I got help from Bette Jane, my younger sister, number four at Tucson High. Majored in education, minored in Spanish. Heard elementary schools needed men, later learned they wouldn't hire minorities.

Did student teaching in Nogales, on the border, then training in Pittsburgh and Flint, Michigan.

Had four kids, three boys close together. Started a masters, getting principal's credentials, thirty hours, classroom teaching, bilingual school.

Joined Mexican American Committee of Educators, Chicano movement, Congressman Raúl Grijalva, activist on school board.

Office of Civil Rights finding, 1972: only two Mexican-American principals in Tucson's sixty-five elementary schools.

Superintendent Thomas Lee covers his ass, phones, "Howe, are you Mexican-American?"

I say, "Always have been."

He asks, "You interested in being a principal?"

I say, "I'd like the job."

He says, "By the way, do you have credentials?"

I say I do.

At his office, he says, "Keep this quiet until the board approves."

Frank Howe

III

Not from Tucson

Dad's family moved from Minatitlán, Veracruz, to Mexico City when he was a child. After his first year of college, he migrated to Chicago, then got his Ph.D. at the University of Illinois and married an Anglo woman from nearby Flora.

Later he taught in the Spanish department at the University of Wisconsin.

I liked Madison, my friends, the snow, being a good student, sandlot baseball and football.

When I'm twelve, winter of grade eight, we move to Tucson. A jolt. Nothing green, desert. While waiting for the school bus, we build fires, warming the early morning chill.

A new friend calls Mexicans dirty, looks my way, says he doesn't mean me. I see what I'm up against, where I have to stand, decide I must re-learn Spanish, must become Mexican-American.

I talk on and on with my grandmother as she cooks chila-
quiles, budín azteca, arroz con pollo. Mama Emilia speaks
no English. In fits and starts, my Spanish begins to flow.

Then I join the Chasers.

Chico Rosaldo

Ornamental Oranges

Never did anything bad except throw those oranges, summer school after junior year. They took us to jail, then the juvie, Mother Higgins.

On the last day of class, Redhead Jerry and a bunch of gringos challenge us to an orange fight.

Early morning, we park on Second, pick ornamental oranges, take backseat out of Ginger's '53 Chevy, fill it and the trunk with oranges, drive to school, throw oranges all over the place.

Moustache, a short Mexican cop, hauls us to jail.

Frank Robles, the lieutenant, says, "Oye, Dick, who the hell brought you here?"

I say, "That guy, Moustache."

Robles challenges Moustache, "What the hell you think you're doing? Do you know they're all under eighteen?"

Moustache says, "Caught 'em throwing oranges, gotta book 'em."

Robles says, "Get them the hell to Mother Higgins."

Moustache warns us, "Don't try to get away."

Robles says, "Don't worry, we know their parents, know where they live. Nobody's going anywhere."

Moustache lectures, "Don't hang out together, bad influence. You'll break a window, enter, become hardened criminals."

At Mother Higgins, Moustache makes us call our parents.

My mom comes by taxi, asks, "What you doing tonight?"

I say, "Nothing, Mom, you told the man I was grounded."

She says, "The man doesn't know what he's talking about. You planned something, que no?"

I say, "Yeah, Mom, we were going to have a party."

She says, "Go to your party, okay? Don't worry about it."

I say, "Okay."

That was it. We did some crazy stuff. For those days.

Dickie Delahanty

I Never Liked You

BOBBY SAYS,

Now that I mention it, Chico, I never liked you. I said, who the hell is this guy? Trying to swim, get records, good grades. Who the hell voted for him?

As we got older, we appreciated you more, were more respectful, realized what you'd accomplished, but at the time you were borderline. I mean borderline.

I don't think we voted anybody out, but you, you were borderline.

CHICO SAYS,

Borderline's the word, the word for me. I was awkward, grew up in Madison, as if from another planet, snow, green, trees. In Tucson, brown, desert, sand, cacti, Mexican border an hour south.

In Madison I competed with friends for A's. A- spelled defeat. I played football in eighth grade. Even then, without telling friends, I aimed for a Ph.D.

Hate to tell you this, Bobby, but I've yet again flubbed my chance to come back at you. In Chaser days I admired how you hard-assed, so quick, so clever, never speechless, always a retort.

Next to you, I felt trapped in silence. What I needed to say, bursting to get out, but not even a whisper. I yearned for a nimble tongue. Yes, borderline.

Bobby Shoumaker and Chico Rosaldo

A Place to Stand

The Navy gives me strength. I'm a classified control yeoman, deal with everything up to top secret.

In Guam I'm the only Mexican in the squadron. Most Mexicans join the Army, Marines, or Paratroopers.

My first day in Guam, somebody gives me a sex book. I'm lying in my bunk in white skivvies reading the book when this guy comes by, looks down, says, "Where'd you get the book?"

I say, "A guy from Ohio, Callaway Lawson, lent it to me."

This guy says, "It's my book. Let me have it."

I say, "No, I'll take care of it with Cal."

I put on my pants, my shoes, my shirt, say to Cal, "This guy's giving me shit, says the book belongs to him."

Cal says, "Yeah? What's wrong with me lending it?"

The guy says to Cal, "Ask me before you go lending my stuff."

I do a Chaser thing for the whole squadron to see, tell the guy, "Here's your book," and boom, I throw it on the ground, say, "There's your goddam book, pick it up. If you don't, what you gonna do?"

I stand my ground, get respect, big time, big time.

Frank Howe

Fiftieth Reunion

We fly New York to Phoenix. Mary drives to Tucson. I nap. Afternoon fatigue from my stroke six years ago.

We reach The Shanty on Fourth Avenue. I walk in wearing our jacket. A roar. We're now (almost) complete, ten here, two not yet found.

Our jacket: *Chasers Tucson,* stitched red letters, tilted martini glass, toothpick in olive, three pink bubbles, one bursting. We sit in patio, October afternoon sun, enormous sky.

Bobby asks me to read my Chasers poem, the one he recited before I arrived. As I read, his sure hand touches my lower spine, firm support, know-how of a neurologist, now retired.

Rocha tells Mary about the first day I drove my family car to school, forgot it, rode home on the bus. "So like you, Chico," he says, wide smile, head tilted back.

He recalls the assembly where they announced my scholarship to Harvard, how proud he felt. I had no inkling. So like me not to hear praise.

Ray lives on the border, two of his children born in Mexico, citizens there. He's been a singer for thirty years, now stands before us, resonant voice.

He belts out Mexican corridos, ballads of love and death. Patio crowd applauds, bartender gifts us pitchers of Dos Equis.

We speak of how Ray ran to defend Jim Sickler who'd been jumped. "Not a fair fight," Ray said. The rest of us ran after him, joined the fray.

Willie put to music verses he learned in my dad's Mexican Culture class. He sang: "I live with flowering songs. I want and desire deep brotherhood, nobility. I yearn for songs. I live in flowery songs."

These verses are by Nezahualcoyotl, fasting coyote, ruler of Texcoco, warrior, poet, author of Flower-Songs.

We recall the fight between Ralph and Henry. Ralph much smaller, more than held his own, landed solid blows, a moral victory.

Louie asks if our lives have ever come to a crossroads. We say nothing. His crossroads was an arrest for possession. The cops stole his van.

Louie decided to devote his life to crime, treated it like a career. "If you're Mexican, you lose," he says. Then he challenges Ralph to a game of pool. Louie wins.

Five of the guys were egged into a fight in Mammoth, came home bruised, their dads laid beef steaks on black eyes.

Guys lust after the waitresses on the patio, flirting, eyes tracing their breasts and asses, impulsive regression to high school.

Delahanty tells of the girl who invited us to crash her party. Her dad came at us with a baseball bat. We scattered. We laugh at how we ran, at what we could have done.

Dickie Cota-Robles says he loved the punch at my parents' parties. Bobby laughs, hard-assing, "You were designated driver, you said you didn't drink."

Delahanty greets me, "Que gusto verte, Chico." I say, "El gusto es mío." Bobby laughs, says, "Chico doesn't speak Spanish."

Bobby says he spoke Spanish before English, he's still not at home in all-Anglo, English-only groups.

Angie says good-bye in Spanish, tells Bobbie and Frank, "Yo creía que ustedes no hablaban español." They take the bait: "¿Cómo crees? Siempre hablábamos español."

Patti talks about grandchildren with my brother, Bob, and his wife, Cris. Bobby, Frank, Cota-Robles, Rocha, and I sit together. We speak, con sentimiento, about our kids and grandchildren.

Chico Rosaldo

• BOBBY SHOUMAKER •

I Was Shaking

Our sons, prison terms for possession, taught us that if we project ourselves from then to now, doing what we did, half of us wouldn't have survived in this society as it is now.

We'd have gotten shot or caught for having a few beers in a car. Something would've happened bad.

Take the summer day we filled Ralph's car with oranges, took handfuls, started throwing in classrooms, unbelievable, unbelievable.

We got nabbed, paid our dues, ended up at Mother Higgins, they phoned our parents. Mom and Dad thought I did nothing bad. Nobody got knocked unconscious by an orange.

Standing at our place in the stairwell, watching girls go by, when Ray saw an Anglo classmate, Jim Sickler, get jumped by a bunch of Mexican frosh.

Ray ran to help Jim, called out, "Come on, not a fair fight." We had a big hoorah, Mexicans against Mexicans.

Next day, the school lawn was packed, guys strutting, as if soldiers in a race war, flaunting chains. Intense, so tense, explosive.

I was shaking, possessed by an urge to run, nobody took our side. "Chasers?" I said, "We don't get on, never heard of them."

By next morning, tension evaporated, left not a trace.

Bobby Shoumaker

Three Months Older

Last day, sophomore year, we crashed Judy's party.

Jumped over the wall, that's when, at that party, Dickie met Patti, now his wife.

I met Kay, my wife, when she was a sophomore, I was a junior.

I'd walk by the door where she was in class, make faces.

The teacher'd come, I'd go running.

That was the first time I made any contact with her.

Then we started dating. Dickie with Patti. Me with Kay.

Patti and Kay lived in the same neighborhood. We'd double-date.

Then Dickie and Bobby begin hard-assing, mock mutual attack.

Dickie says, "He's like three months older than me."

Bobby says, "God Almighty, he always brings that up."

Dickie says, "You're three months older in March, but the neatest thing is I married Patti in 1964."

Bobby says, "April 4, 1964."

Dickie says, "Right. And you married Kay . . ."

Bobby says, "August 29, 1964."

Dickie says, "And we're still together."

Bobby says, "I was copying him. I always idolized the guy. Jesus."

Dickie says, "Shows how strong our family is."

Dickie Cota-Robles and Bobby Shoumaker

Guys on One Side

We were destined to be who we are. Bobby was always studious, even if he played the joker.

I marvel at Bobby's becoming a neurologist, Koenig a psychiatrist, Frank Howe a teacher. Chico, your studies were fantastic.

We were into sports, bond of being competitive, got along super well, no egos, wouldn't let you have one, Bobby destroyed them with the songs he liked. The Big Bopper, "Hello, Baby, you know what I like."

In school everybody envied how we were tied so close. We would be invited to crash parties, the girls would say, please crash, liven up our party.

Remember that blonde who lived on the south side of Broadway, at El Encanto Estates, very pretty girl?

We went to her place, looked over the patio wall, guys on one side, girls on the other.

That was no party, and they all knew it, so we jumped the wall and started dancing with the girls.

The Anglo guys said, "Let us introduce you." I said, "You want to do something? Go sit down."

After that we left, but we were invited to crash. It was neat, you look back. Wow!

Dickie Delahanty

In the School Yard

I'm an Anglo, wanted to be a Chaser, but they never invited me. Only club I wanted to join that wouldn't accept me.

The Chasers stood at their place on the stairwell watching girls go by. They looked out the window, saw Jim Sickler get jumped by a few Mexican frosh he offended at the rodeo parade a day before. They ran out, made it a fair fight.

Next day, everybody crowds shoulder to shoulder in the school yard, trying to make it Anglos versus Mexicans versus blacks, but fail, race not yet rigid at Tucson High.

John Warnock

Erased

I suppose I started it, phoned Dickie Cota-Robles, said I was coming to our class of '59 reunion, asked if the Chasers were getting together. He said nothing, simply started the search.

Next I hear, Angie writes, coy, asks if I remember her. She reminds me: we went steady for three years in high school.

Says she saw Rocha and Willie Cocio looking for Chasers who've drifted apart, fallen out of touch, but hope to get together soon. She thought I'd like to know.

After our gathering, Rocha mails me a photocopy of the *Campus Chronicle* article. One photograph is blanked out. Willie Cocio's been erased, even though he helped locate the guys. You are or are not a Chaser.

Chico Rosaldo

You Won't Do Well

I wonder whether in high school we separated from Anglos or they segregated us. Neither Irene, rodeo queen, nor Clara, student council, kept their distance, but many of us did.

Guidance counselors played a role. When I registered for ninth grade, I requested algebra, but my counselor asked if I knew what it was. I said I took it in eighth grade.

He asked for my report card, but I didn't have it. He said, "Let's put you in general math. If you do well, we'll put you in algebra next year." No more discussion.

I knew no better, just went along. The class was all Mexicans. I remember Bobby Saenz, gorgeous, but he couldn't add or subtract.

I was bored, passed only because Eddie López and I competed for grades. Next year, algebra, all Anglos, all freshmen.

Counselors treated us as if we were dumb, tracked us away from college. When I told my counselor I was going to college, he discouraged me, and I thought, he just doesn't know. I'm smart.

English class, all Mexicans. Mr. Egan, the teacher, asked, "Who's going to college?"

I raised my hand.

He said, "You won't do well, your vocabulary's poor, you'll be placed in English X, never get out."

Tears rolling down my cheeks, I walked away.

Angie López

◆ ANGIE LÓPEZ ◆

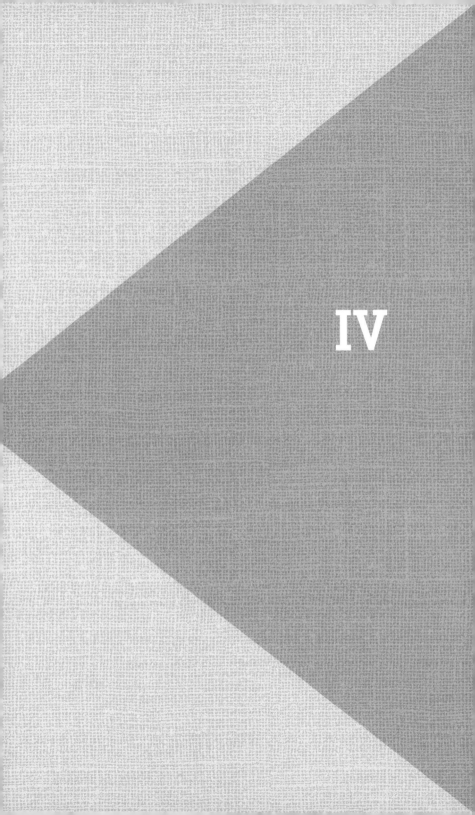
IV

Observing

I flopped the first time I tried to hard-ass. Failure shut me up, made me feel like I did the day the word "elefante" eluded me, as if my tongue had been pulled out by the root.

In my family's '51 Dodge, I drove across town, east to west, house to house, picked up the guys, hard-assing the entire trip. I remained mum, under a bushel basket, no sign of me.

> Bobby says, "Now that I mention it, Chico, I never liked you. I said, who the hell is this guy? I don't think we voted anybody out, but you, you were borderline."

Restoring my Spanish left me unable to master another language, the catlike rapid swats of hard-assing. Instead I listened with all I had, became a quiet guy, laughing, being an audience, observing. Comprehension way ahead of speech.

> Dickie says, "He's like three months older than me."
> Bobby says, "God Almighty, he brings that up every time. I always idolized the guy."

For me, hard-assing became the ultimate test of being a Chaser, of being Mexican-American. Fifteen years later I found I could hard-ass with West Indian masters of the art.

> A West Indian says, "I want to visit your housemate. Are you her guard dog?" I say, "Who wants to know? I've been hired to keep you away. By your mother."

Marinating in years of silence, all was not lost.

Chico Rosaldo

Never a Fighter

I don't remember the Vikings, nor the Gaylords, don't remember their jackets, don't remember their being there.

I guess we knew there were gangs back then, just can't recall the others, but I sure remember the Chasers, the jackets, you were so visible, your spot in the stairwell.

You were involved in everything else, not many class officers, but a lot of athletes, a unifying thing for the Chasers was sports, a sociability about the group.

In my own mind I was a wannabe, would love to have been invited, knew I wouldn't be, was never a fighter.

My role at Tucson High, breaking up fights, a goodie. I remember a couple of girls fighting in the hallway, stepped between them, broke it up. Like I said, I was a goodie.

One thing I'd still like to know, can I join the Chasers? Can I at least have a jacket?

John Warnock

Papá y yo hablamos

PAPÁ DICE,

El Delahanty me dice que le da vergüenza hablar conmigo en español. Piensa que no lo habla bien.

DICE EL CHATO,

Le intimidaste. ¿Qué le dijiste?

PAPÁ DICE,

Le pregunté que si me entendía cuando le hablaba. El dijo que me entendía sin problema. Y le dije que yo también le entendía perfectamente. Le dije, si nos entendemos así, seguiremos hablándonos en español sin nada de vergüenza. No hay porque hablar inglés.

Chico Rosaldo

Dad and I Talk

DAD SAYS,

Delahanty says he's ashamed to speak with me in Spanish.
He thinks he doesn't speak Spanish well.

CHATO SAYS,

You intimidated him. What did you say?

DAD SAYS,

I asked if he understood me when I spoke to him. He said he
understood, no problem. I said I understood him perfectly.
I then added, if we understand each another this well, let's
speak Spanish without shame. We don't need English.

Chico Rosaldo

• DICK KOENIG •

You Were or Were Not

Evenings I helped Ralph do janitorial work at the Alianza Club. I was fortunate to have been a Chaser, and am grateful to Ralph for the invitation, made me the man I am today. I've tried to be a loving man who knows how to cry, yet is able to hold his own.

I'd been too protected when I joined the Chasers. Do you remember what you did, Chico, when we played pick-up football? You slammed me, a clean blow. I'll never forget. Toughened me.

Unconditional acceptance by the Chasers meant the world to me. Being Jewish, I knew something of the bias you guys dealt with.

It was all for one, one for all. You were or were not a Chaser.

Dick Koenig and Chico Rosaldo

Raw Eggs

We Chasers need an initiation to become who we are, but have no one above or below, no hierarchy.

We draw straws to pick the initiates. I'm one of the four being initiated. That leaves eight in charge. One of the eight says, in their initiation, the lettermen made Art Acosta wear a dress to school for a week. Four of us shudder.

At Ralph's house, raw eggs smash, hurt like rocks, hoses drench. They dress us in gunny sacks, blacken our faces with charcoal, spray our heads with Burma-Shave.

They parade us through bleachers at a baseball game, girls point, snicker.

At Johnnie's, they order burgers and set the jukebox to humiliate with our exit dance, "The Stroll."

Past the cop, past the cash register, without paying. Bobby escorts, grabs a handful of toothpicks. Cop says, "You took a lot." Bobby says, "Lots of teeth."

We dive in water at Sabino Canyon, mock fight, four against eight, one punch lands hard. Wet eyes are masked by night, but the dark air carries a Chaser's sob.

Bobby yells, "This is an initiation. No grudge here. Don't throw real blows. Be cool."

Chico Rosaldo

My Brother Raúl

My brother Raúl was given Dad's name. Dad was a boxer, trained me and my brother to hit a punching bag, put us in a ring. We boxed without hurting each other. We were six or seven.

Dad would ring the bell. One time Raúl turned around. I punched him. My brother was upset, and Dad said, "That's a good lesson, never turn your back on your opponent."

Much later I learned my brother was the protector for other guys, like Bobby Shoumaker was for the Chasers. Raúl respected you guys. When I began dating you, Raúl said, "The Chasers are really neat, treat Chico right."

When he was sixty-three, I sat by Raúl's deathbed. For two weeks we held hands, talked, cried, sang tender farewells.

Angie López

I Remember

CHICO,

I've read *The Chasers*. It's good, it's great. It brought back memories.

I remember you, Chico, your beautiful girl, Angie. I remember all the guys, full of testosterone, their girlfriends— gorgeous girls.

One night I picked a fight at the VFW on Broadway. Always protective, Shoumaker said, "Rocha, let me handle him." I backed out, let him take the guy on.

We went to the back alley, expecting Bobby to make quick work of the guy.

"They call me the Fork," the guy said, as he started shadow boxing. Oh shit, nobody knew he was a pro. He began jabbing Bobby's face. The fight was over before it started. The Fork stood, untouched.

We'd go to drive-in movies, hide three or four guys in the trunk, free admission.

We'd stop at drive-in diners, Johnnie's on Speedway and the Crossroads in South Tucson where the carhop would set up a tray. We'd order French fries and pitchers of beer. We were seventeen, probably looked fifteen.

Four of us went to a dance in Mammoth, a town of five hundred, mostly miners and cowboys. They were mean, ruthless, loved to fight, beat the shit out of us. We're lucky to have survived.

The kidding among Chasers—only among Chasers—was brutal. Calling each other "stooge," we toughened up by hard-assing (a term not used nowadays).

I still cherish our camaraderie, the friendship. Wearing our jackets, putting on parties, made us feel like we belonged.

I remember Chaser days as if they were yesterday. God watched over us—still does. We remember Andy.

So long, Chasers. I love you all. You are great men. We beat the odds!

Thank you, Chico, for your book of poems, this requiem. God will repay your love for the Chasers of Tucson High School, 1959.

Good-bye.

Richard Rocha

• RICHARD ROCHA •

An Old Story

1867

Tucson School District One was founded. Fifty-five Mexican boys were in the school.

There were three school committee members: Mr. Allen, an Anglo merchant; Mr. Oury, a former mayor, an Anglo; Mr. Leon, a politician of Mexican descent who lasted but a year.

EARLY 1950s

Robert Salvatierra became the third school board member of Mexican descent since its founding.

LATE 1970s

Minority groups sued District One for segregating black and Mexican-American students. They found patterns of segregation by race in elementary school boundaries and in assigning students and teachers.

1978

All parties agreed to court oversight of the school district.
The district had neither complied with the desegregation
agreement, nor eliminated vestiges of past discrimination.

AMONG EARLY PIONEERS

Expatriate southerners were prominent in Tucson. Their
legacy: slavery and segregation. No one taught students this
old story.

Chico Rosaldo

I Am a Chaser

After gathering for our fiftieth reunion, an afternoon beer led to late breakfast the next day, and on and on, almost comic repetition. An urgent need held us captive. We couldn't keep ourselves from re-reunioning.

As we told stories—Chaser days—late fifties...time flows—in and out of me...Chico then...Professor now...always Chato...the depth and opacity of a dream. Where and when did I begin and where did I end?—a memory, a dream, a feeling—forgotten chatter gets closer, clearer...an invitation to the past from this moment.

In the grip of stories, I came to know my debt to the eleven guys who had my back, who sustained, who taunted, who toughened, who carried me through teenage years to my emergence.

The passage of time gifted me certainty. I am a Chaser. He is a Chaser, so is he, he really is a Chaser, and on and on, almost comic repetition. The ease of my acceptance by the Chasers mirrored the ease of my acceptance of the Chasers.

My doubt about belonging dissolved. The value of what we lived, the world we created, affirmed. We remembered and re-remembered.

We told and re-told stories, one by one, together, multiple versions, one weaving, different hues, resilient fabric.

Chico Rosaldo

My Dad Died When I Was Six

I had to hustle, stay alive in this world, but hey, I'm kicking, two houses, two cars, lots of bills.

After graduation I lost track of the guys—two years in the army, plus reserves, liked it, except simmering summer camp, July, Fort Irwin, Mojave Desert. Drove an M 48 tank, one big bulky chunk of metal. Left the service in 1962.

I started in the moving business with Farrugut Bags and Transfer—six years there, made good money, dollar fifty an hour, that was fifty years ago.

In the morning we'd unload meat, deliver, little stores— Chinese and Mexican. I was a helper, learned to pack, drive a truck.

Then Tucson Warehouse, labor to sales, I'd ask their needs. Should movers pack? I'd quote prices, people'd question: is this price firm?

They'd say, "The garbage man comes to my house, movers can too." I'd say, "No, no, no, these trailers are huge."

A lot's changed since I was a young man, trucks are harder to handle, thirty-five-foot trailers, then forty, now fifty-three.

I retired seven years ago, moved to Pinetop, bought land there twenty-five years before, saying, "One day I won't be able to put this truck in reverse."

Now I'm an independent contractor, back in COD sales, bring my Palm Pilot, ask, "What's going? What's not?" Make sure a tractor-trailer can get in there.

That's pretty much my life, married late, at twenty-seven, my wife, Marie Laos, was twenty. People said, "Won't last. They're gonna cut your electricity off." Fooled 'em—been married forty-five years.

Freddie Ochoa

Packager

His life had been remarkable.
—JOSE MONTOYA, "El Louie"

We eat supper at Frank's. Louie's silent. After dessert, he tells about his life flying Cessnas filled with weed from Mexico and Jamaica to just over the Arizona border.

The danger's addictive rush kept him in the business.

He found the best places for menudo in Santa Fe and the south valley of Albuquerque. In Boston he once played poker with Ted Turner (yes, *that* Ted Turner) whose bets were so big Louie folded.

His guardian angel was a woman who studied law to get justice for her unjustly imprisoned husband. Louie gave her money, supported her through law school.

He was no snitch. His first time in prison, he was well taken care of, given joints he then passed on to people who cleaned his cell.

When he returned to the business, he dropped down the totem pole, transporter to packager. He shrink-wrapped three-hundred-pound blocks of marijuana to load them in car trunks.

Before he got busted the second time, his expensive cars and fancy entrance gate were asking for trouble. Once his boss was arrested, he knew he'd be next.

Knowing he was being watched, he stood in his front yard, and smoked a fine joint. He knew he'd get no joints that fine in prison. The court ordered him to rehab and took a year off his prison term.

In Florence penitentiary, his second prison term, he served as the elder in a Native American sweat lodge. Fifty people had his back. Even so, prison was hard this time.

He is too old to continue as before. Because he never snitched and is out of the loop, he can now safely quit the business.

After Louie finished talking, we sat stunned, silent. Bobby said, "Louie's shown we were hot air, not guys on the wild side."

Louie Dancil and Chico Rosaldo

◆ LOUIE DANCIL ◆

Sure Hope We Can Enjoy
a Few More Years

Andy Contreras died last year. His family had him buried in his Chasers tee-shirt. They said his Chaser years were his best. His jacket will be on a hanger at our get together Saturday night.

Years after high school he turned to drink, developed diabetes, went blind. We'll drink a glass of tequila to Andy and our memory of his harmonica's wail at our last gathering, his final gift.

From high school I remember his long poem. He took me aside and paced as he recited from memory, urgent need for me to listen.

At first he looked down, then in my eyes. He was shy, uncertain, yet fiercely proud, as he revealed his art. Evoking San Diego in his rhymed verse, he began, "I rode a shark to Balboa Park," and much more.

Chico Rosaldo

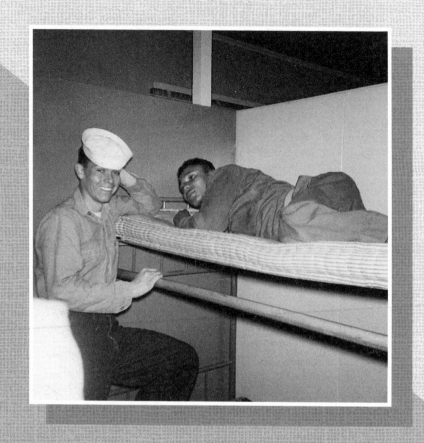

• ANDY CONTRERAS •

Acknowledgments

Mary Louise Pratt, most of all. And for her photo of John Warnock. Marty Correia, manuscript adviser; my brother Bob Rosaldo who videotaped my interviews with the Chasers and friends; Dan Chavez, for most of the contemporary photos; Lorie Novak, for the photo of a Chasers jacket; Gisela Fosado, exceptional editor.

• CHASERS REUNION, JUNE 2018 •

• DICKIE COTA-ROBLES •

• LOUIE DANCIL •

• DICKIE DELAHANTY •

• RAY ESCALANTE •

◆ **RALPH ESTRADA** ◆

♦ FRANK HOWE ♦

◆ DICK KOENIG ◆

◆ ANGIE LÓPEZ ◆

◆ NEAL MANNING ◆

• FREDDIE OCHOA •

◆ RICHARD ROCHA ◆

• RENATO ROSALDO •

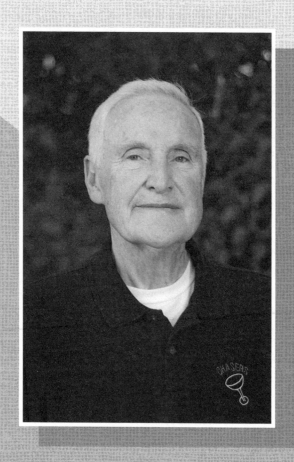

• BOBBY SHOUMAKER •

• JOHN WARNOCK •